TRESPASSING IN EDEN

*Reflections on
the Christian Faith, Church and Ministry*

by

Walter D. Wagoner

Published by
Two Bytes Publishing, Ltd.
1995

Cover Art:
Front cover: Pictured is the Round Hill Community Church, Greenwich, Connecticut
Back Cover: Pictured is the Yale Divinity School, New Haven, Connecticut

Copyright © 1995 by Walter D. Wagoner
All rights reserved.

ISBN: 1-881907-24-4 (soft cover)

Two Bytes Publishing, Ltd.
219 Long Neck Point Road
Darien, CT 06820

PRINTED IN THE UNITED STATES OF AMERICA

DEDICATION
With Love to Fafie

Foreword

These pages contain over-the-shoulder reflections, gazing out the study window at various experiences: fifty years in the ordained ministry, college and military chaplaincies, seminary administration, foundation work and parish care. Here are but vignettes, a pastoral miscellany, hints, musings. I ask the reader to regard these observations as the first words in a lively conversation.

Hamlet's Polonius, giving the advice of the paternalistic elder to the young, is not my model. Rather, I have written this to bring to the surface opinions and convictions which for years have been and still are seeking adequate formulation and which will profit from the reader's evaluation.

W.D. W.

Trespassing In Eden

Foreword v
Table of Contents vii

I. THE FAITH 1
God's Strongest Competitor 3
Supernatural Selection 5
The Religiously Neutral 7
Creeds (One): Basic English 9
Creeds (Two): On Knowing The Unknowable 11
Faith's Flying Buttresses 13
A Tailor-made Parable 15
Godly Form: Human Function 17
The God Of The Commonplace 19
Atheism, God And The Boson 23
Who Is A Christian? 25
Is Jesus Over-qualified? 27
Christian Vision 29
The Stethoscope Of The Spirit 32
The Final Theological Choice 36
Christian Suicide 38
How Long Do We Live? 39

II. THE CHURCH 45
Honeymoon Ecumenicity 47
How To Join A Church 50
How To Empty A Church 52
Wedding Tales 56
How Holy Is Communion? 59
Ante Mortem: The Quick And The Dead 61
Post Mortem: The Christian Valedictory 63
Second-Hand Samaritans 65
God's Troubadours 67

II. THE CHURCH (cont'd)
- God's Alter Ego 69
- A Bodiless Church 71
- Peripatetic Piety 73
- On Being An American Christian 75
- A Good Word For Do-Gooders 78
- Vox Populi, Vox Dei? 80

III. THE CLERGY 83
- A Word To And From The Pulpit 85
- Ministerial Mobility 87
- Sex And Sermons 90
- My Real Bible 93
- The Christian: Professional And Amateur 95
- One Armed Justice 97
- The Minister's Fatal Sin 99
- A Christian Commencement 101
- Continuing Competence 103
- Greener Fields And Ministerial Salaries 106
- Benefit Of Clergy 109

IV. SERMON: Fifty Years A Minister 111

V. Conclusion and Author's Biography..................119

THE FAITH

"Not only the historical existence of a man called Jesus, but the credibility of the story of Jesus in its main features belong to the essence of the Christian faith. Christian faith cannot arise without an historical picture of Jesus."

Emil Brunner, <u>Revelation & Reason</u>

GOD'S STRONGEST COMPETITOR

When Sunday attendance is poor, when laity are hard to arouse, we clergy brood and ask ourselves why more people do not take God and the church seriously. Our answers are stock-in-trade: "Mammon and Sex have taken over" ... "Nests are being feathered" ... "Self-centered hubris is out of control" ... "The Big Bang and Black Holes have ousted the creator God ..." "Too many human woes."

My own answer differs. I affirm that God's strongest competitor is ordinary "muddling through": the amount of time and energy we are forced to expend simply to stay afloat. I refer to the distractions of everyday life, our thousand little preoccupations. As the Parable of the Banquet has it, "I have bought five yoke of oxen, and I am going to try them out, please accept my regrets." In short, keeping up with inflation, hanging on to the job, shopping for cottage cheese, and trying to find time for recreation are God's strongest competitors.

A delightful anecdote illustrating what God is up against concerns a young husband with an attractive wife. Her addiction was new clothes. She spent too much on dresses, and they were in debt. So she agreed not to buy anything without first talking it over with her husband. Nevertheless, one day she went to town and came back to surprise her husband with a new gown. The husband complained, "But, dear, you promised me." She replied "I know I did, but the devil tempted me." He answered, "You should have said, 'Get thee behind me, Satan.'" "Oh," she replied, "I did, and the Devil whispered, "'It fits so beautifully in the back.'"

Thus, after years of fretting about God's competition, I conclude that it is not bad times or personal disaster that pushes God off center stage. It is, rather, what Saul Bellow described as "The Great Noise" .. the sounds of daily living, of paying for the car, the din of politics and the need to save money for a two weeks vacation at Lake Wawatonka.

SUPERNATURAL SELECTION

I am not a morbid person, but I do read with more than passing interest the obituary columns in both the morning paper and in my college alumni magazine. Who has died? Who lives?

I mention that doleful habit and those questions because lately I have been thumbing through a list of dead or dying gods - a pantheon of <u>Who Was Who</u> among the deities.

The obituaries of the gods pose two unavoidable questions: "Why do deities die?" and "Will the God of the Christians survive?"

But, before further theological autopsy, here are a few names of dead or dying deities:

1. Tasai-Shen: Chinese god of wealth.
2. Enki: Chinese god, half-goat, half fish.
3. Ababinili: Fire god of Chickasaw Indians.
4. Blodenwedd: Flower-faced goddess of Gaels.
5. Dab-Lha: Warrior god who sits on Tibetan shoulders.
6. Ganapiti: Four handed Hindu god.
7. Ma: Mother goddess of the Hittites, worshipped by prostitutes.
8. Taaroa: Tahitian god living in cosmic egg.
9. Zeus: Chief god of ancient Greeks. Athena sprang from his forehead.

Christians assert that the God whom we worship cannot die. By definition, we insist, our God, the universal God, is eternal. This God was not created by human imagination. Humans, of course, might not pay attention to God. They often deny God but, Christians affirm, God exists quite independently of human attitudes. If God were dependent on human thought, God would not be God.

With that basic Christian assumption in mind, it is appropriate to ask the inevitable and relevant questions about the life-span of deities. For example, will the God of the Christians be, in Darwinian terms, "fit" enough to survive the competition from other theological species? Is "survival of the fittest" a fruitful way of studying comparative theologies? Which attributes must one's God possess in order to survive? If there is "natural selection", is there also "supernatural selection"?

To begin the conversation, I propose two minimal qualifications for a God to survive:

First: God and the related theology must be able to survive the most searching critical examination by philosophers, theologians and scientists. In the long run neither atheism or theism will sweep the world. Christian theology, however, must be able to hold its own in open debate.

Second: God must be concerned for and compassionately involved in our human situation. The universe may not be human centered but a God who is only a metaphysical construct, with no connection to our human scene, will quickly perish.

I submit that a God without the two foregoing attributes will soon be found in the obituary column.

THE RELIGIOUSLY NEUTRAL

I well remember a short story which piqued my ministerial interest to an exceptional degree. It was a vignette of a suburbanite man who on Sunday morning is washing the family car, prior to going on a picnic. He hears a distant church bell, pauses for a split second, then finishes wiping the headlights.

That split-second pause deserves our close and sympathetic attention. I know that man well. "One of my best friends" is the man washing his car at 11:00 a.m. on Sunday. Let's look at him for a moment from a religious perspective.

That suburban neighbor is neither an atheist nor an agnostic. He is neither for religion or against it. He is religiously neutral. He just doesn't think, other than for an occasional minute, about religion. Oh, once in an off-moment he may wonder about death or about the creation of the universe. However, he is a bench sitter who is not interested in the playing fields of religion.

To understand the mind of such a man or woman it is helpful to cite the following letter which a minister received. The minister had just paid his Welcome Wagon pastoral call on a new arrival in the town. A few days later came this note: "Thank you for your visit. Let me try to explain our situation with regard to possible membership in your church. I am 65 years of age, retired after an active life, and very happy. My wife is six months younger than I. We have been married forty years very happily. We have never attended church. We have never said a prayer. Neither of us believes in life after death. We believe in making this world better. Without seeming egotistical, I believe we have succeeded. We are not hampered by creeds, but stare life squarely in the face. So, in all honesty, and with appreciation for your visit, we really don't know what church and religion has to offer us. Sincerely."

St. Mark's gospel tells us that on one occasion Jesus was "amazed at their non-belief". Such non-believers must have been more of a surprise in Christ's religious culture than in our secular one. We are surrounded by many who simply do not have God, Christ, church, Sunday School, choir, creed, or Bible on their agenda.

As a believer, I am uneasy with all these neutral neighbors. To me, they are like the man who was out fishing in his small boat when a sudden squall blew up, threatening to drown him. "Lord," he prayed in his panic, "you know that I have not troubled you in twenty years and, if you only get me out of this, I'll not bother you again for another twenty."

But that is patronizing laughter on my part. After all, the neutral person doesn't make fun of me. So, the best advice I can give to my missionary instinct is to enjoy the friendships of the "neutral", while not hiding in what and whom I believe.

CREEDS (ONE):

BASIC ENGLISH

George Bernard Shaw left a substantial portion of his estate to promote a simplified vocabulary. Shaw poses a challenge to Christians who have inherited traditional creeds based on the opaque philosophical language of the fourth and fifth centuries A.D. For example, The Nicene Creed of 325 A.D.: "I believe in one God, the Father Almighty, Maker of heaven and earth, and of all things visible and invisible: and in one Lord Jesus Christ, the only begotten Son of God: Begotten of his Father before all worlds, God of God, Light of Lights, Very God of very God: Begotten not made: Being of one substance with the Father .."

Given the heresies and the christological debates of those centuries, The Nicene, Chalcedon and Athanasian Creeds were magnificent accomplishments. Those creeds served the church well, particularly in the attempt to explain the Trinity.

Christian faith, however, is in God and in Christ's relationship to God. Our faith is not in a creed, old or new. Creeds are direction signs, referents to be studied. They are not verbal icons. More pointedly, the great creeds, including those of the Reformation, need to be rewritten in contemporary language.

Therefore, I see the necessity for two types of creeds, each in current language. First, each congregation or denomination is strengthened by devising its own creed as a regular part of its public worship. Such a creed should be as inclusive as possible, reflecting both the heritage and the current convictions of the local parish. Just as we change hymnals from time to time, so these local creeds call for occasional revision. Second, each individual Christian needs to articulate a personal creed. None of us believes exactly what any one church creed asserts. We assent to the church creed because it is a fair effort to represent the most inclusive theology of the parish. At the same time it is not dissimulation for each person to articulate more precisely his or her Christian viewpoint.

There is an experiment well worth trying some Sunday morning. The minister will announce: "Instead of the offertory and the sermon this morning the ushers will distribute paper and pencil. For the next half hour there will be silence as each of you writes the central convictions of your personal faith. It is yours alone to read and keep. By the way, you are not permitted to open the pew Bible, the hymnal or the prayer book until you have finished. Do your best. Above all, remember that one's faith does not consist in a list of things not believed."

CREEDS (TWO):

ON KNOWING THE UNKNOWABLE

We Christians make the most extraordinary claims about our knowledge of God. We assert that God has a beneficent will, that God is our creator and that God's purpose is known most fully in the life of Jesus.

We are so accustomed to such astounding affirmations about the nature of God that it is very much in order to back away from such declarations in order to recognize their sheer enormity. Many outside the church would say that our Christian portrayal of God is a bizarre example of human egotism. We at least should listen seriously to those who deliberately and thoughtfully prefer to be silent about the nature of God.

Christians have not been content with such a silence. Christians would not be here if the silence had not been broken. We believe that the Bible interpreted with scholarly caution does reveal the nature and activity of God. We claim, further, to find clues about God elsewhere in history: in biography, the arts, science, philosophy, nature and intuition.

All Christians affirm that the crucial knowledge of God is to be seen and felt in The New Testament. A majority of Christian churches affirm the absolute divinity of Christ: that Jesus of Nazareth was God in the flesh. I, with a minority of Christians, prefer to affirm that, insofar as it is humanly possible for a fully human mortal to show forth the purpose and nature of God, Jesus did so.

The final mysteries of divine being are so beyond our comprehension that we and our creeds must be restrained from glibly assuming detailed knowledge of God. Honest theological speculation is undergirded with such cautionary words as "maybe" and "hope". Nietzsche voiced the necessary restraint in his bitter warning: "I like not these coquettish bugs who in their insatiable desire to smell of the infinite make the infinite smell of bugs". He was speaking about those whose religious faith had turned either into ideological fanaticism or into a mawkish familiarity with God. Christians affirm unique convictions about God. We voice important and resonant sentences about life and death and deity. But we are human and God is God. The distance between God and us, however shortened by Christ, is so vast that humility, finger to mouth, must be our constant attitude.

FAITH'S FLYING BUTTRESSES

The Cathedral of Notre Dame in Paris provides a beguiling analogy for personal religious faith. Notre Dame's gothic walls are supported by flying buttresses. Centuries of wind and weather have found their match in the angled power of those mighty piers.

The last time I saw Paris it occurred to me that my faith, too, has many supporting buttresses. The related and disturbing question is, "How much of my faith would be left standing if the outside supports were to collapse?". Parenthetically, the atheist and agnostic should ask the same question of their philosophical architecture.

My Christian faith has numerous "outside" supports. There is the backing of the church. Its history, worship and members bolster faith in God. There is also a significant degree of support provided for most of us by our parental, family allegiance to the faith. Further, in the United States there is still wide cultural underpinning for the place of religion. The majority of Americans profess religious faith. Such factors comprise a solid and substantial series of buttresses.

The ordained clergy have additional supports. I have had the encouragement and example of able fellow clergy and teachers, of seminary formation, of church organization. Nor can any minister afford to overlook the public regard given in measurable degree to the ordained person.

Finally, and most difficult to assess correctly, are those buttresses afforded to the faith and hope of clergy and laity alike by decent physical health and a modicum of material well being. Those are the buttresses which Job lost. They are supports which I still enjoy and for which I am grateful.

I will not push further the Notre Dame Cathedral analogy. It is, however, healthy that each Christian arrives at that telling moment when he or she ponders the proportionate mixture of personal "interior" conviction with "exterior" supports.

I am unsure how to weigh the role of flying buttresses in the construction of my faith. I cannot easily separate the inward and outward sources of my faith, so intertwined are they. I only can be thankful for the additional help which I know has been given to me by exterior principalities and powers.

A decisive and telling analysis of the respective roles of personal and exterior forces in the shaping of my faith would be revealed if I were suddenly stripped of health, comfort and church supports. I pray that I shall never be in such a religiously naked and frightening predicament.

A TAILOR-MADE PARABLE

I cannot avoid or escape any of the parables of Jesus. However, I suspect that, like everyone else who takes them seriously, there is one parable which fits perfectly. It speaks to my particular personality, inclinations and excuses. It is, in that sense, "my" parable.

I refer to the Parable of the Wedding Feast. It bedevils me with questions about my Christian maturity. That is, one major sign of personal maturity is the realization and the admission that I cannot have life exactly the way I want it to be. An infant, an immature child may howl and cry for immediate and complete self-satisfaction. You and I, in our mature moments, know better.

I am an immature Christian whenever I blame God for life's incompleteness, for not creating a perfect humanity. *My immaturity consists in forgetting how much freedom of choice God has given me.* Because I am so reluctant to recognize the extent and the results of my freedom, I find the Parable of the Wedding Feast to be a word of Jesus that speaks to me with a grim particularity. That parable fastens on me; it will not let me out of its clutches.

The parable is Jesus' way of telling me that God hopes that I will gladly accept God's invitation to come to the feast of the Kingdom: that festive gathering of all those who love God and seek to do God's will. And yet, that same God has given me the freedom to refuse the invitation and to go about whatever business I choose.

Well, many a century has come and gone since Jesus told the Parable of the Wedding Feast. The oxen are gone without a trace, and the Lord lives. The property about which the man was so concerned has changed owners a thousand times, and the Lord lives. The bride and groom are voiceless, and the Lord lives.

As long as I live that parable will haunt me.

GODLY FORM: HUMAN FUNCTION

The architectural adage that form follows function is equally true of our conceptions of God. The verbal form we give to God reflects, in varying degree, our personal functions: what we do and who we are.

There are many obvious examples of the shaping of God close to our own images.

In a hymnal widely used in the 1930's, a time when the brutal labor-management, anti-union fights were at their height, was this line in a hymn: "Let Jesus no union card deny!"

Liberation theology portrays a God who is on the side of the poor and oppressed.

The feminist movement has God free of all patriarchal motifs.

Afro-American theologians emphasize God as a liberator of the enslaved.

More personally, the God I worship bears clear evidence of my own liberal, white Protestant background. It is a God I first dimly discerned in a comfortable Missouri suburb. That youthful vision was enlarged and criticized at the various seminaries I attended. However, as much as I would like to transcend the particular culture and bias of my life, I cannot fully escape a mixture of my image and God's.

Theoretically, we Christians assume that we are strict monotheists worshipping the Lord God, Creator of all cultures and all humans. Functionally, however, that pure vision of God is adulterated with our values, prejudices and human limitations.

A telling way to clarify how we tailor-make God to our specifications is to tell a true story about an eclipse of the sun. Years ago a film company desired to photograph a total eclipse and to show it, for profit, in movie houses. The trouble was that at the critical moment the eclipse site was closed over by fog. It was then decided to return to the Hollywood studio and there manufacture a total eclipse and sell it as the real thing. The fake, however, was exposed. During the studio preview there appeared across the face of the sun the dim words, "General Electric".

Your name and mine are to be seen across the face of God. Our task is to make them as dim as possible.

THE GOD OF THE COMMONPLACE

I understand that if our memories were fully retrievable we would lose our minds, not being able to absorb so much from the daily past. But I do wonder how the days and months of yesteryear would look to us if we had total recall?

Some people claim that in moments of acute danger, or near death, they have seen "my entire life pass in review".

I am not at all sure that I, even under tranquil conditions, want to see my entire life pass in review. It would require censoring and far too much of it would be repetitive and commonplace.

The very notion of a life review reminds me of the lady who each year on her wedding anniversary secretly went to the basement of her home, ran backwards the home movie of her wedding, and left the basement feeling single again.

Suppose for a moment, however, that we could remember the days of our lives, all of them. We would be startled to find that ninety-nine percent of those days have been predictable, commonplace. By commonplace I do not mean that our lives have been uninteresting. I mean that most of our days are composed of ordinary events: getting dressed, brushing our teeth, going to work, shopping, answering the phone, eating meals, attending church, going to committees, driving the car, reading a book.

I, for example, have had a very interesting but largely commonplace life. It is obvious by now that I am never going to be invited to dinner at Buckingham Palace. I am still waiting for Jack Nicklaus to invite me to the first tee at Augusta. Another year has come and gone without a word from the Nobel Prize Committee.

Most of life is run-of-the-mill. Thus, if God is to be a reality in our lives, God will have to be sought, remembered, prayed to and thought about in the midst of daily life.

So it is, therefore, that I cite that curious biblical story about Naaman and his leprosy.

Naaman, the Commander in Chief, the hero, was suffering from some skin ailment. He wanted God to cure him instantly and dramatically. And so he went to the Prophet Elisha in the expectation that Elisha would dance and pray and wave his hands and call out to God to cure Naaman: "Behold, I thought the prophet would come out to me and stand and call on the name of the Lord our god and wave his hands and cure me." Elisha, however, simply said to Naaman, "Just go down and wash yourself in our own River Jordan and you will be cured." Elisha was trying to disabuse Naaman of his belief in a God who would only be known through astounding miracles.

Naaman is any person, of whatever religion, whose God is essentially pictured as a super magician, exercising power in melodramatic ways.

Such a God is far distant from our every day world. The God of spectacular thunder and lightning and stupendous miracles is not a God who lives where we are ninety-nine percent of the time. Where do we live? We go through the days putting a dime in the parking meter, rushing about in shopping malls, attending committees, talking with neighbors, eating pizza. We swim in quite an ordinary river, our own River Jordan.

For most of us God must be found, thought about, prayed to in the course of daily life: family, friendships, civic tasks, solitary moments.

In 1620 the ship, Mayflower, on its way to New England, had an average rate of speed of three miles per hour. Those pilgrims kept their faith during that slow, commonplace voyage. Undoubtedly, some pilgrims might have believed in God with more fervor if God had blown them across in one day.

There is, I suspect, a bit of Naaman in each of us. We do wish that a great thundering event would reveal the presence of God. In effect, we now and again wish that Elisha would come out and call on the name of the Lord and wave his arms and cure violence, illness, drug use and old age.

There is a story about a little boy who is afraid of the dark. One evening his mother says to him, "I want to sweep the floor. Go out on the porch and get me the broom." Well, it's very dark out on the porch and the little boy says, "I'm afraid to go out there cause it's dark and something's going to get me." His mom says, "Go ahead. You don't have to be afraid. God is out there." Well, the little boy thinks about this for a minute and then opening the door he calls out, "If you're out there, God, bring me the broom."

The desire for a God with a broom recalls a movie about Jesus. In the crucifixion scene the director insisted that Jesus' chest be covered with vaseline and thus brightly reflect the rays of the sun. It was grotesque. The director shared Naaman's view of God.

If we do not seek and worship God, and permit God to find us, in the ordinary mainstream events of our lives, we will starve religiously. These lines make the point:

> "If God were suddenly to make a blind person to see, we would stand, wondering all, and call it a miracle: But that God gives with lavish hand sight to millions we stand and say, with little awe, God but fulfills the Natural Law."

The teaching and parables of Jesus emphasize that God is to be found while sweeping a room, praying alone, helping a stranger, scattering grain, attending a wedding, walking to Jericho, teaching at a well, conversing at a meal; the plain acts of everyday life. Further, as we know, Jesus often told his disciples not to tell anyone about acts of his that they interpreted as miraculous, as spectacular.

We will grow in faith, or atrophy in faith, in the midst of the plain and simple annals of daily living. That is where we find the God who gave us life and who makes commonplace life worth the living.

ATHEISM, GOD AND THE BOSON

It is necessary to admit the attractiveness of atheism. Any minister who denies that is not seriously dealing with the important temptations. Nothing invigorates a theistic faith more than a persuasive, intelligent atheist. The siren calls of atheism are always heard in the minister's study. Pretending to be deaf does not diminish their voices.

Atheism comes in many guises. There is the anti-clerical atheism so often found in countries where church and state are too closely conjoined. This atheism demands that "the last priest be hanged in the entrails of the last king". This rejection of God is also a rejection of an ultra nationalistic, often corrupt church.

There is the formidable moral atheism based on the persistence of evil and human suffering. It is the atheism found in the cancer ward or at the graveside of a child. This atheism either denies or refuses to worship a God whose creation is so cruel.

There is philosophical, cerebral atheism. Can there be an absolute? Where is any empirical proof for God? Does religious language have meaning? Is faith in God a psychological projection?

At this writing, the form of atheism most in the headlines concerns the debates of particle physicists and cosmologists. One does not need to be a sophisticated mathematician to get the drift of the debate.

A recent column by a Nobel physicist argues for a subsidy (rejected by Congress) of the super-collider because it would further reveal the nature of the subatomic universe, explaining the universe, he affirms, "in terms which do not need any recourse to faith in a divine creator.*[1] Another Nobel Laureate makes the same point, indicating that if and when the theoretical "boson" particle is verified, "we can write the universe-explaining equation on a T-Shirt".[2]

Over against such atheistic claims are the arguments put forward by an impressive list of theistic scientists. To cite but one: Dr. Owen Gingrich, Chairman of the Department of Astronomy at Harvard: "Creation is a far broader concept than just the moment of the Big Bang. God is the creator in the much larger sense of designer and intender of the universe".

I see no evidence that the tension and oppositions between theism and atheism will ever be settled conclusively. However, the minister who does not attempt at least to keep current with the shifting forms of the debate will lose credence in increasingly well educated congregations.

---

[1] Steven Weinberg, N.Y. Times Op-Ed, March 8, 1993.

[2] Leon Lederman, The God Particle, Houghton Mifflin, 1993.

WHO IS A CHRISTIAN?

Imagine that you are a passenger on a train in India. The Hindu woman seated next to you finds out from your conversation that you are a member of the Christian Church. She then, without desiring to argue the point, asks, "How do you define a Christian? Who is a Christian?"

A definition that is acceptable to all Christians is impossible. That is so because in the New Testament there is such a variety of portraits (not photographs) of Jesus. It is from that gallery of painting that each Christian derives his or her basic definition of a Christian. Any responsible definition, therefore, labors under the necessity to take into account at least the prevailing interpretations of those portraits, plus the latter christologies.

There is one definition which begs the question. Namely, "A Christian is anyone who claims to be one". That is too slippery.

I prefer to get at a fairer definition by asking, "What is the essential conviction among those who call themselves Christians?".

My considered reply is this: Christians believe that in the Jesus of The New Testament, there is portrayed that person who, more clearly than any other in human history, personifies and reveals the nature and purpose of God.

Such a definition is, I submit, the largest possible tent covering the greatest number of self styled Christians. To be sure, additional convictions would be added to suit the taste of this or that individual Christian. Such a person might emphasize the resurrection, or the ethic of Jesus, or his saving grace.

I define myself as a Christian. Jesus has seized my mind and imagination and muscle as none other. The New Testament portrait of Jesus is so compellingly-life-like and so commanding that my eyes, which often linger long in front of other human portraits, always refocus on Jesus Christ as the most superb and moving human embodiment of God's attributes.

IS JESUS OVER-QUALIFIED?

Throughout vast areas of American Christianity Jesus of Nazareth is sent running on hundreds of trivial errands. He is shamelessly exploited. For thousands, Jesus has become the theological victim of Gresham's law which reminds us that cheap money drives out the sound. Similarly, the cheap mishandling of Jesus quickly weakens his true nature and his valid qualifications. I illustrate.

Jesus is a bumper sticker: "Honk, if you love Jesus". Jesus is a T-Shirt savior. His name is chanted as an "open sesame" to solve any and all problems. Jesus is used as an ego-booster: "Jesus is my co-pilot". Jesus is an icon, a rabbit's paw. Jesus this and Jesus that until we feel like shrieking, "In the name of Jesus Christ, can't you let him alone for an hour or two?".

The good name of Jesus is co-opted for partisan political platforms, as a forecaster of world events, as the predictor of the next Armageddon, as the local crime and drug buster, as guru and as restorer of lost causes. Jesus is not, I beg to submit, qualified for most of the household chores we wish him to do.

Jesus is not qualified as a business reference or as a character witness. Jesus is not qualified as a credit reference or as a corporate outside director. Jesus is not qualified as a modern geologist debating evolution or as an astrophysicist arguing the Big Bang. Jesus cannot prevent bankruptcies. Nor can he raise an academic average the night before an exam.

27

Re-reading my sermons I realize that I also have often used the name of Jesus too carelessly. I am afraid that I have, almost unconsciously, given my own opinions the imprimatur of his name. After all, the sermonic use of the name "Jesus" gives a ring of authority to whatever is being preached, especially if the minister is at a loss for credibility. Too freely invoking Jesus is a temptation which the preacher finds it hard to resist.

Therefore, I would plead that we refer to Jesus with restraint and dignity. Jesus is a friend, but he is not a buddy. I would plead that our commitment to him be based firmly on who and what he is, the revealer of God and the embodiment of the best in human nature.

I would blaspheme were I to set any limit to his influence. But I am disturbed and angered by the frivolous way in which we so often fling his name about.

Is it unfair to wish that once in a while we simply would let Jesus be - let him alone? As Martin Luther wrote, "While I sit here drinking my glass of Wittenberg beer the gospel runs it course.".

CHRISTIAN VISION

A Gallup Poll asked this question: "Which is the worst affliction that can happen to your body?" Blindness was mentioned five times more than any other ailment. I therefore ask these questions: "What is Christian vision?" "What is religious blindness?"

As prelude to an answer, consider the uniqueness of our physical eyes. They are protected by frontal lobe bones, eyebrows, eyelids, tears and fast blinking reflexes. Each second that our eyes are open one billion pieces of information are sent to our brain. Our eyes can sense seven million gradations of color. Further, our physical eyes see what we want to see. We tend to overlook that which does not interest us. The quip of a parishioner is to the point:: "My minister's eyes I've never seen, though light from them may shine. For when he prays he closes his, and when he preaches, mine."

What is Christian eyesight, Christian vision? It is the ability, insofar as we are able, to look at life and other people through the eyes of Christ. His perspective adds to our religious depth perception. Jesus knew how to position himself so that he could see clearly both the surface of life and the human heart. He possessed dual vision.

Christian vision not only sees Main Street and the people living and dying there, it also sees the hopes, fears, problems, joys which animate those citizens on their pilgrimage from birth to death.

Dual vision, of course, is not limited to Christians. The Christian eye, however, has its special receptivity and insight. There is a particular compassion, a strong sense of seeing the world under the aspect of eternity.

Dual vision is difficult and in great demand. There is symbolic coincidence in that the two books most stolen from The New York City Public Library are Bibles and books of etiquette, evidencing desire both for the inner and the outer eye.

Accurate, interpretative eyesight, either worldly or spiritual, is not easy. Here is an example of an extraordinary failure of worldly eyesight:

In 1858 a scientific expedition passed through that part of our country we now know as the Grand Canyon. A young lieutenant by the name of Ives made this entry in his report: "This region we last explored, the Grand Canyon, is, of course, altogether valueless. It can be approached only from the South, and after entering it there is nothing to do but leave. Ours has been the first and doubtless will be the last party of whites to visit this profitless locality. It seems intended that the Colorado River, along the greater portion of its lonely and majestic way, shall be forever unvisited and undisturbed."

For us not to take advantage of the eyesight and insight of Christ is comparable to the nearsightedness of the explorer, Lt. Ives, in his opinion of the Grand Canyon.

As Christians, then, we seek to amplify our human vision with the extraordinary eyesight of Jesus Christ. The First Letter of John puts it perfectly:

"We write to you about the Word of Life, which has existed from the very beginning. We have heard it, and we have seen it with our own eyes. Yes, we have seen it, when Christ's life became visible we saw it."

THE STETHOSCOPE OF THE SPIRIT

In Omaha, Nebraska, this ad appeared in a local paper: "For $8.00 per hour I will listen to whatever you wish to say. Absolutely no confidences broken." The woman who placed the ad was swamped by those who had, as one customer put it, "No ear in the world." The ad underscored our need for caring personal attention.

The ability to listen sensitively does not come naturally. I think that these curious outcroppings on my head, these ears, must have been the last of my senses to mature. My other senses: sight, touch, taste and smell, don't give me as much trouble.

The title of this essay refers to our stethoscopic ability to listen, not only to the muscles of the heart, but to the throbbing of the inner life: ambitions, disappointments, joys, ecstasies, hope and grief. Jesus cultivated his inner ear to a remarkable degree. The New Testament is filled with vignettes of Jesus stopping to listen carefully to a rich young ruler, a woman at a well, a tax gatherer, a frightened disciple, a cripple, a blind beggar and many, many others crying for personal attention.

Over and again we see the Son of God, with such a tragically short life, usually pursued by crowds, yet stopping to hear one individual pour out grief, remorse and anxiety. Jesus gives his full attention. He doesn't give the impression that he is late for a supper in Bethany. He makes it unmistakably clear that the person to whom he is listening is important to God and that Jesus wishes to help.

The stethoscope of the spirit enables us to hear what is behind or underneath the voice of the person in need. Sensitive attention tries to discern what is really being said and how we best may respond.

In the seventeenth century a very talkative nun suddenly realized that she had not been much of a listener. She wrote these words in her diary:

"Lord, thou knowest better than I know myself that I am growing older and will some day be old. Keep me from the fatal habit of thinking I must say something on every subject and on every occasion. Release me from craving to straighten out everyone's affairs. With my vast store of wisdom, it seems a pity not to use it all: but thou knowest, Lord, that I want a few friends at the end."

Having quoted that, I grant, of course, that we can't always be listening intently. Much conversation is casual and not a signal for therapy. Many people, most of the time, have nothing startling to say. A Roman Catholic priest who once served as Chaplain to a convent came up with a widely quoted remark: "Listening to confession at a convent is like being stoned to death with popcorn."

However, I know of no one who, at one time or another, does not wish to be listened to intently and seriously.

I happen to believe that in matters of this sort men tend to be more deaf than women. As one man remarked to another, "My wife says that I don't pay any attention...at least, I think that's what she said."

Here is an excerpt from a letter which a sixteen-year old wrote to his parents:

"Remember when I was about six or seven, and I used to want you just to listen to me. I remember all the nice Christmas things you gave me. But the rest of the time I just wanted for you to listen to me like I was somebody who felt things, too. But you said you were too busy."

The biblical counterpart to that cry is this: "Now Martha was distracted by her many tasks...Mary sat at the Lord's feet and listened to what he was saying."

Paying close attention, whether it be Christ listening to others or we listening to Christ, brings to mind this memoir from the diary of Princess Marie Louise, niece of Queen Victoria.

"Saturday last I had dinner with Prime Minister Gladstone. He talked to me all evening. When I came home I was convinced that he was the cleverest man in all of England. The very next evening I dined with Mr. Disraeli. He listened to me all evening. When I returned home I was convinced that I was the cleverest woman in all of England."

LISTEN to this:

"As he approached Jericho, a blind man was sitting by the roadside, begging. When he heard a crowd going by he asked what was happening. They told him, "Jesus of Nazareth is passing by." Then he shouted, "Jesus, Son of David, have mercy on me." But those who were in front sternly ordered him to be quiet; but he shouted even more loudly, "Son of David, have mercy on me." Jesus stood still and ordered the man brought to him, and when he came near, he asked him, "What do you want me to do for you?"

Surely, it is no coincidence that the person who listened so well to people is the same man who heard God so clearly.

THE FINAL THEOLOGICAL CHOICE

Using melodramatic pedagogy, let me ask this question: "If we Christians knew for a certainty that in fifty years all forms of human life would be wiped out by a natural disaster, not by human fault, would our present faith in God be changed?".

As preface to my own answer, I submit that there are two types of Christian believers whose answer would be quick and predictable. The first is that Christian who is determined to keep faith in God no matter what. For this person no event will eliminate faith in God. God was, is, and will be even if humanity disappears. The second type of Christian will instantly surrender God. For this person God is a comfortable addendum to a comfortable life. God's reality depends upon a minimum of health and well being.

But what of my faith in God if I knew that my grandchildren and billions of others would die because of a collision with an asteroid or because of a radical change of climate?

I have no idea if my faith would survive. I would like to think that I do not worship God because God created this universe primarily to sustain human beings. I would like to think that my faith in God does not depend upon my personal circumstances. I would like to think that my emotional panic at the thought of destruction would be counterbalanced by a thanksgiving to God that we humans have had a good long run of it. I would like to think that there are probably other forms of self conscious life in the universe who worship God. I would hope that there is a life after death in the presence of an eternal God.

Such a planetary holocaust, putting an end to our heritage, to my grandchildren and all humanity, might create so much anger and hysteria within me that I might shake my fist at a God who, for me, no longer existed.

I just don't know how my faith would fare.

CHRISTIAN SUICIDE

There are, so I read, serious warning signals given off by a person truly tempted to suicide: constant talking about it, suggestions on how to do it, possession of weapons, intense depression and even inherited predisposition.

The obvious analogy comes to mind. Are there, any clues and signals which indicate that a Christian may be tempted to religious suicide?

There are such warnings signs. These do not lead inevitably to self-afflicted apostasy, but the symptoms are not to be lightly disregarded.

One ominous warning sign is found in the parishioner who is a chronic complainer about church life. For this person there is nothing within or near the church which is worthy of praise. The sermons are always dull, the sexton can't shovel snow, the Sunday School is in disarray, Bible study is not directly correlated with the Dow-Jones, the hymns are unsingable, etc., etc. That parishioner's faith is almost certainly destined to self-immolation. I have no solution. Neither prayer nor sympathy, nor counselling (deep or shallow), will avail. The only hope for the Church is that the parishioner will leave town and that the suicide will occur elsewhere.

A second type of potential Christian suicide is embodied in the parishioner who is absolutely certain that "one religion is as valid as another" and that no matter where we are or who we are, all pilgrims gather finally at the gate of the same kingdom. Moses, Buddha, Radakrishna, Mohammed, Jesus, Aquinas, Mary Baker Eddy, Joseph Smith, Jonathan Edwards and Pat Robertson are on the same cosmic highway, if only a few feet apart.

This parishioner cannot conceive that some religions contradict others, that varying visions of good and goodness are real and that one believer's faith is another's poison.

When swallowed, such theological mush will cause Christian suicide.

HOW LONG DO WE LIVE?

I recall that marvelous cartoon showing an angel on Cloud Nine asking an angel on Cloud Ten: "Do you really believe in an heretofore?" I reverse the question and ask what all of us ask: "Do you really believe in an hereafter?".

The vast majority of the world's religious answer that with a resounding affirmative, even though there is much variety in portraying what life after death is like. There is, for example, a pointed difference between Socrates' vision of the immortal son and Christ's affirmation of an individual self-consciousness able to recognize God.

Judaism, Islam and Christianity affirm eternal life. So did the ancient Egyptians. So did Plato and Aristotle. So have scores of other philosophers, scientists, artists and theologians.

Christianity, in keeping with the teaching of its founder, embraces life after death as one of its basic beliefs. Saint Paul, indeed, puts in unequivocally: "..as all have died in Adam, all will live with Christ...if for this life only we have hoped in Christ, we are of all people most to be pitied."

The belief in life everlasting is not a dry as dust, pie in the sky belief. It is an emotionally powerful, dynamic, motivating hope and affirmation, overflowing with anticipation and consolation. No back of the hand, academic brush-off should be given to this conviction.

We recognize, obviously, that there are those who do not believe in any form of eternal life or immortality. The non-believers and skeptics assert that when this body dies there is no more human life, no exit. The empiricist maintains that if life eternal cannot be demonstrated it cannot exist.

As for the argument that life after death is wishful thinking, I can only submit that whether we wish for it or not is beside the point. Life eternal is true or not true, quite independent of our wishes or our denials.

C.S. Lewis has an interesting comment; a variant argument:

"Creatures are not born with desires unless satisfaction for those desires exists. A baby feels hunger. Well, there is such a thing as food. A duckling wants to swim. Well, there is such a thing as water. We wish for love. Well, there are fathers and mothers, husbands and wives, sweethearts and friends. However, if I find in myself a desire for a final and complete meaning of life which no experience in this world can satisfy, the most probable explanation is that I was made for another world where the meaning of life can be experienced."

Admittedly, you and I stand, when contemplating the grave, before a vast mystery.

Oliver Wendell Holmes in a funeral oration put that mystery in poignant form:

"Brethren, we pass from the abyss 'I know not whence', into the abyss 'I know not whither' and as each of us in turn leaves the light someone who loved him or her utters a cry, and then the great silence prevails once more."

There are two major reasons, among others, which cause me to affirm the Christian view of life after death.

First, the very existence of such fantastic life forms on this planet alone, from the amoeba to the cerebral cortex, is to my mind and heart as miraculous and breath taking as life after death. God's creative power is as much evident before death as after. The God who can create this universe surely can preside over our lives after death.

The second reason for affirming life after death is based on my faith in God's nature and my trust in the wisdom and experience of Christ. "In my father's house are many mansions; if it is were not so, I would have told you."

I agree with the seventh century monk, The Venerable Bede:

"Human life is like the flight of a bird. The bird flies out of the shadows through an open (birth) window into a lighted room (this world where it remains for a time. Then it darts through the open window at the other side of the room (death) into the semi-darkness again. We can dimly perceive, because of the life of our Lord, through both those windows."

I conclude with this expression of my faith. Because of what Jesus was and what he declared about life after death I believe that when we see God we will be in a presence of a familiar friend. When we see God we will not say, "Who are you?" We will exclaim, "So it was you all the time!"

Today, this moment, is the near edge of eternity. You and I did not know what awaited us when we arrived in this life, and we do not know exactly what awaits us in the next. But we do know that God had a hand in our coming, that God is with us now, and that God will not leave us when we return to our Creator whose parish is the universe and all of time.

THE CHURCH

> *"The church is called to be the place where God's purpose for the world becomes visible in history as a sign to the world of its own destiny."*
>
> Owen Thomas, <u>Introduction to Theology</u>

HONEYMOON ECUMENICITY

Answer this question: What have been the two or three most influential Christian experiences in your life?

As the reader will expect, I have my own reply at hand. The twentieth century ecumenical movement. has been one of the most profound Christian experiences of my life.

William James long ago pleaded that each of us find the "moral equivalent to war". To a marked degree I found that in the formation and progress of the World Council of Churches and similar national and local ecumenical organizations.

It was an experience arising out of both theological conviction and personal participation. In seminary I had been active in "The Inter-Seminary Movement" - a scholarly scouting expedition across institutional boundaries. I was privileged to be the host administrator for the Second Assembly of the world Council of Churches in 1954 at Northwestern University. I also was a delegate to the Third Assembly at New Delhi. I was fortunate enough to attend sessions of the Second Vatican Council. Close friendships across many confessional and denominational lines added zest and vision.

It is a present temptation, of course, to indulge in ecumenical nostalgia, the rust of memory, about the joys of that surge toward Christian unity, roughly from 1948 to 1970.

Those who today profit from the accomplishments of the ecumenical movement cannot imagine how hermetically sealed off were the churches and seminaries even fifty years ago. Denominations and theologians often were case studies in invincible ignorance.

The current lull in ecumenical activity betrays, in part, the simple loss of memory. An analogy to our current ecumenical attitudes, vis à vis past accomplishments, is to cite the manner in which we today have never known or have forgotten what hospital wards were like before the invention of antibiotics. We take those medical advances for granted, with hardly a sigh of gratitude. So, too, for our forgetful attitude about past ecumenical progress.

I do not romanticize the ecumenical movement. It has its share of conflict, misunderstanding, pride and abrasive personalities. Nevertheless, our present ability to rub elbows with Orthodox prelates, to listen to Anglican scholars and Roman Catholic authorities, to talk theology with Lutherans from Malaysia, to worship with Southern Baptists from North India, to trade tales with missionaries in Kenya, to listen to black church members from South Africa, to pray with Copts and Presbyterians, to share communion with Methodists, to support seminaries with students from a dozen denominations is the result of one of the most astounding movements in Christian history. And most of it has taken place in my lifetime.

It is inconceivable that the Christian churches now active in the ecumenical movement would revert to the former isolation.

The current situation is like a marriage that has moved beyond the honeymoon era and which now must find continuing satisfaction in the joys and sorrows of the shared years ahead.

It is time, in any event, for all of the churches to renew their marital vows.

HOW TO JOIN A CHURCH

Statistics in today's paper inform me that the United States is a very religious land but that more and more of its citizens are "independently" religious, seeking God outside the church or the synagogue. I would like to hear the reasons for that trend. Let me describe the two major types of persons who do seek God <u>inside</u> the church.

The most fitting analogy is to compare potential church member to two types of swimmers alongside a pool - the church. Each type wishes to swim. The first type of souls pound their chests, shout loudly and plunge heartedly into the water. The second type, hugging thin epidermis, tentatively enter the pool inch by inch and only after careful consideration give the final gasp and swim.

Most of the parishioners I knew are in the second type. They are those who approach the church one toe at a time, staying in the shallow end as long as possible. Indeed, just when I think that they are about to swim they will bolt and run. But finally they do return and they do swim. They have sampled the worship, the sermons, the creeds. They have looked at the building, analyzed the minister and the profiles of the members. If they have children, they have diagnosed the Sunday School. By the time they come before the congregation to join the church, the minister is as nervous and limp as a college admissions officer in April.

The other group, the plungers, are a minister's delight. These persons come to the church's pool eager and smiling. They are determined to swim, signing up at once for study groups and committees, taking umbrage if they are not promoted to the Trustee Board within two years. In short, they soon become Life Guards. They frolic with the youngsters in the wading pool; they splash water on forty-year members and throw the minister off the high dive. There they are, toweling their goose bumps. Welcome to the deep end.

HOW TO EMPTY A CHURCH

I write with no little authority on this subject. I know that it is far easier to empty a church than to fill it. Indeed, if anyone about to be ordained or about to be installed as a minister to a new church were to ask me to speak to the occasion, the following rumination is what I would shoot over the bow of the newly launched minister.

The usual assumption is that a full church is the great desideratum and the conclusive sign of the church's Christian mission. Most of the time that may be a fair goal. Not all of the time, however. There are, according to my convictions and prejudices, too many churches which are jammed tight but where the gospel is badly distorted. Be that as it may, I proceed in the hope that a full church is a deserving goal. To that end, I propose three primary reasons, among many possible, why churches have empty pews.

First: An empty church results when the life of the church (public worship, music, education, social action) does not give primary focus to God and Christ. There are hundreds of programs and institutions which meet our political, social and recreational needs. Such programs, however, are the secondary obligations of a vital church. The church has no justifiable reason for existence unless it helps us mortals in our quest for the divine and the eternal. Too many churches lose members because the secondary has displaced the primary. What I mean is illustrated in the story of a man who made a visit to The New York Public Library. He passed the sculptured lions keeping their vigil at the front steps. He walked between the renaissance pillars. He saw the display cases, the mounted stamp collections, tapestries, busts of benefactors, rest-rooms, checkrooms and elevators. Finally, in desperation, he turned to a staff member and demanded "Where are the books?" Empty pews always result when the church does not meet the primary desire of those who come through its doors wondering "Where is God and Who is Christ?"

In this noisy, strident world there is a tremendous human need simply to be able to see and to hear Jesus: Our raucous world reminds me of Casey and Riley who were sight-seeing in London, riding on top of one of the double-deckers. The din and rattle of the city were almost unbearable. When they came in sight of Westminster Abbey with its chimes bursting forth in glorious melody, Riley leaned over to Casey and said, "Don't those bells invigorate you?" Casey replied, "You'll have to speak louder, I can't hear you?" Riley again, "Don't those chimes give you a sense of reverence?" Casey, "You'll have to speak louder." Riley, "Don't those pealings take you to Galway to the days when the world felt young, and God was in his heaven?" Casey put his mouth close to Riley's ear and said, "Those damn bells are making such a racket, Riley, that I can't hear you."

Well, there is a terrible din and racket in our daily world; and it takes some doing simply to stop long enough to hear or see Jesus. It is through exposure to him that faith comes. This is why it is important to read the scriptures, to avail ourselves of the sacraments, to sense his presence in other people and to be open to his spirit in the clamoring world around us.

Second: A church empties when the minister is too far ahead of the congregation.

By "ahead" I do not mean that minister is a superior person or that the minister is showing more insight than the congregation. Rather, I am suggesting that it is lethal when the minister's ideas and goals are so different from those of the congregation that there is little hope for resolution and consensus. When there is too much distance between clergy and congregation some ministers believe that they are either martyrs or neglected prophets. That is rarely the case. The more usual situation is that the minister simply doesn't realize that in order to lead a church one has to be close enough to the congregation in order to understand where it is on various issues. Effective leadership results in tension, not in separation.

Third: A church suffers when the minister is not able to win the trust and friendship of the congregation. Such acceptance and regard is based on respect, on mutual caring. This shared confidence takes time. Trust occurs when there is a constant, natural face to face relationship. The minister must not hide behind professionalism or dignity of office. Friendship abounds when confidentiality is kept and when a genuine, loving sensitivity is demonstrated, day after day.

This mutual respect between clergy and laity is not founded on agreement in all matters of theology, social protocol or political persuasion. Neither one party or the other has to be all things to all people.

In summary, perhaps I have given too much prominence to the role of the clergy in emptying or filling churches. There are many other sad reasons why churches fall empty: when gossip gets out of hand, if personalities clash, if partisanship divides governing bodies or when finances are not cleanly handled.

It is a tribute to the churches that so many succeed in staying alive and vigorous, with active members, not only in a world of competing faiths and ideologies but also with congregations that represent a variety of personalities and loyalties.

WEDDING TALES

A common experience in the ministry is to be approached by a couple who admit to having little or no church affiliation but who fervently desire to have a church wedding with all flourishes and trumpets. Even though this request may reflect their opinion that the church is only a bit of proper stage scenery, after discussion with the man and woman I usually agree to officiate. It is a step in the right direction.

I regret not having kept a complete log of all the marriages at which I have officiated. It would be either shocking or reassuring to know how many marital bondings have stayed glued together. I think of that verse from the Beatles:

"When I get older, losing my hair
Many years from now,
Will you still be sending me a valentine,
Birthday greetings, a bottle of wine?"

Having often been asked to give a wedding homily, I have discovered that such talk does not come easily. In part, that is because in the nervous excitement of the ceremony the bride and groom seldom can remember what was said. There is partial compensation in knowing that some in the congregation listen intently. What should one talk about? It is intriguing to ask that question of friends. The predictable reply mentions "good communication" or "compromise" or "forgiveness". Such suggestions are on target. A psychiatrist friend of mine who has specialized in marital counseling maintains that the most important factor contributing to a satisfactory marriage is the willingness to accommodate, to adjust, to be flexible, to bend in the winds of wedlock. All such advice is very helpful. A Christian homily, however, goes beyond such admonitions. The binding power of shared faith is crucial.

I am much put off by wedding ceremonies and parties which are vulgar displays of money, forms of catered exhibitionism. Far too many times I have seen thousands of dollars spent lavishly more to impress the guests than to honor the bride and groom. Often the bride's parents go absolutely berserk, as if the primary purpose of the wedding were either to display social standing or to counteract the lack of it.

All clergy are conversant with the crises at weddings, with ceremonial gaffes. I had seen bridesmaids faint, ring bearers wet their satin pants. One wedding, held on a lawn near the horse paddocks, resulted in the bride, a skilled rider, bringing her favorite filly down the grass behind her father and herself...a maneuver which had not been mentioned in the rehearsal. The beast behaved perfectly. On another occasion the groom fainted twice, and the ceremony was completed with bride and groom seated and with the bride's mother in catatonic shock. Even worse, I once attended a wedding where the bride refused to come down the aisle.

As one who dislikes melodrama, I no longer include the ancient rubric: "If there be anyone here present who knows any impediment to this marriage, let him now speak or forever hold his peace." There is enough tension without voicing that. One minister friend of mine did ask that question. It was answered by a woman with a boy in her arms who stood up in the rear of the church and shouted, "I do."

There are few events in the life of a minister which are as gratifying as the marriage of a man and a woman who are truly in love, who have thought and prayed about their wedding and about whom, when the ceremony is over, one says "That's a perfect match!"

HOW HOLY IS COMMUNION?

Is the Sacrament of Holy Communion, the Eucharist, a <u>sine qua non</u> for Protestant Christians? Is its celebration crucial to the power and propagation of that tradition?

Holy Communion is a faith enhancing habit of my personal and communal devotion. That is, of course, not surprising in the case of a minister. Experience, however, has persuaded me that a sizeable minority of Protestants do not regard this sacrament as a necessary element in public worship or in the life of the Protestant tradition. Somewhat against my will, I am constrained to believe that such Protestants would continue to be active, professing Christians if, to put it starkly, there were no eucharistic observance.

It may be that I am drawing too sweeping a generalization from my personal history, but it is clear to me that for many parishioners Holy Communion is a distant third or fourth in importance, behind prayer, sermon, scripture and music.

Far too many Christians receive Communion by rote and with meager understanding of its role in Christian history. A small minority do not wish to receive Communion. Further, to my knowledge, few Protestants view the observance of Holy Communion as a necessity for salvation or as an absolute prerequisite for Christian identity.

To go without Holy Communion is not to assume that one's faith is only cerebral, without the emotional bonding of a shared Sacrament. The usual Worship Service contains many elements in addition to the purely rational: song, prayer, architecture and other symbolism, as well as the bonding of shared worship.

My conclusion then, is two-fold. First, Holy Communion should be celebrated regularly. It is not to be dismissed casually by an avant-garde liturgist. Second, Protestants who do not view this sacrament as central and crucial should have no guilt feelings. Their piety and discipleship can still be vigorous.

ANTE MORTEM: THE QUICK AND THE DEAD

Years ago I was a guest in a Benedictine Abbey in southern Indiana. One night, visiting a monk in his room, I remarked on a ceramic skull and a crucifix over his cot. Quietly I was told that both were constant reminders that someday he would die.

We Protestant clergy, on the contrary, sleep soundly in a bed next to an alarm clock. There are no eyeless skulls, and our crosses have no dead Christ impaled on them.

In my church and social circles it is considered morbid and, worse, in poor taste to talk about death. Therapists also confirm that "mortal anxiety" is a severely repressed syndrome. It is worth noting that churches sponsor scores of conferences on everything from "The Gospel of John" to "Christians in Mid-Life Crises" but pay very little attention to death. The closest we get to that topic, for the most part, is a discussion of euthanasia or a recital of the psychological cycle of post-death traumas. I do not exaggerate. We are strong about life before death and life after death, but death head-on is avoided. That is, how many church sponsored seminars have been held on "How Do You Handle The Fact That <u>You</u> Are Going To Die?". One fortunate exception to such neglect is the ministry of hospital chaplains.

Thus, I stare at death down life's near or far horizon and try to be honest about my feelings. Is it possible for me to be accepting of and at home with death? Not with death in general but with my death.

If I were in dreadful pain or mental agony, I might well accept death. At the moment, however, in my seventies, I increasingly resent the certainty of my dying. As T.S. Eliot put it, "I see the skull beneath the skin".

I cannot fathom Shakespeare's aphorism: "The stroke of death is a lover's pinch which hurts, and is desired". Not only am I dismayed that the delights of this world will be mine no more, I am miffed that this world will have to get along without me. Quelle dommage!

Intellectually, I have known that my death is the price I pay for my birth, and that the ticket is one way. Emotionally, the task before me is to accept my death with some degree of serenity. I do not find it easy. At this moment, I, like so many, cannot say "Come, Sweet Death".

> "We continue to share with our remotest ancestors the most tangled and evasive attitudes about death, despite the great distance we have come in understanding some of the profound aspects of biology. We have as much distaste for talking about personal death as for thinking about it; it is an indelicacy, like talking in mixed company about venereal disease or abortion in the old days.
>
> At the very center of the problem is the naked cold deadness of one's own self, the only reality in nature of which we can have absolute certainty, and it is unmentionable, unthinkable."
>
> "The Lives of Cell", by Lewis Thomas

POST MORTEM:

THE CHRISTIAN VALEDICTORY

A Roman Catholic friend once told my wife and me, with much laughter, of visiting a funeral parlor to say a prayer for her deceased Uncle Ted. She wandered accidentally into the wrong chapel at the funeral home. She knelt before the open casket, looked up and gasped out, "That's not Ted".

That incident caused me to confess contritely that I have conducted funeral services where there was little indication as to who was being prayed over. The memorial service was routine and impersonal.

I write this as a plea for us, the living, to design thoughtfully, in cooperation with the minister, our own memorial services. That final rite, that Christian valedictory is intended to be not only the church's last word for family and friends; it is also to be the final message from the deceased.

It is appropriate, while we are living, to indicate in writing our firm intentions about the funeral; music, scripture, prayers, eulogies, even the flowers.

You and I can give our funeral service at least as much thought as we do the preparation of our Wills. The funeral service will thus reflect who we were and what we, at the end, passionately deem worth the celebrating. It is not an act of pompous egotism to prepare an Order of Worship which reflects our values, our loves and our faith. Those who survive us and who attend our funerals will deeply appreciate the candor and intimacy of such a funeral.

I would hope that the funeral would include, as previously intimated, a forthright word of our own about what we most deeply believe. With similar logic, the printed Order of Worship ought to include a detailed obituary. We are not simply observing a Christian witness to life and death: We are also celebrating a specific individual, unrepeatable life.

Lengthy funerals are self-defeating. Prolonged labor at our birth is enough. There is no need to overdo our exit from this world. Long funerals cause grateful attention to be replaced by fidgety restlessness. Anyone of whatever reputation can be accorded full honors in well less than an hour.

One or two eulogies well delivered by appropriate persons will suffice. Too many such tributes make for sentimental wordiness and invite the maudlin.

I do wish that the ghoulish ritual of "Laying Out" the deceased in an coffin at the funeral parlor or church would disappear. How grief is alleviated by such a custom eludes me. That exhibitionism verges on necrophilia. I realize that there are counselors who maintain that open caskets during a funeral help us to be more realistic about mortality. That argument is as fallacious as insisting that the parents of a bride and groom won't really believe the couple is married unless the parents also go on the honeymoon? I have blinked at many a casket and found thereby neither a surer affirmation of my mortality nor any catharsis for grief.

SECOND-HAND SAMARITANS

According to the IRS, more money is given each year to religious organizations than to any other category of tax exempt bodies.

In Protestant parish churches tax exempt dollars are solicited to cover the annual church budget. Such budgets, typically, are divided into two major divisions: monies solely for the parish church and, second, monies which the parish church gives to charities.

The percentage of the total budget allocated to outside charities usually varies from five to twenty five percent. Thus, in a church with an annual budget of $300,000 the money given to charity will vary from $15,000 to $75,000.

I propose a more sensible alternative to such second hand charitable giving. This alternative will result in more money being given to benevolences as well as encouraging a more personal and active interest in such charities by the donors.

I recommend that the annual church budget cover only the expenses of the parish church and its denominational obligations. The charitable giving would be done by church members giving directly to good causes of their own choosing.

Under the prevailing system the parishioners, you and I, are second hand Samaritans who permit a second party, the church benevolence committee, to decide where to allocate our charitable dollars. In such a situation we, unlike the biblical Samaritan, may not even be on the same road to Jericho with the man who was robbed and beaten. This is not to say that charitable dollars presently given by churches are wasted; it is rather to maintain that each of us is a true Samaritan when we, not a deputized surrogate, are personally involved.

Writing checks to an intermediary donor only weakens our sense of responsibility. Second hand giving makes it less likely that we will take an up-front interest in the organizational receiving the donation.

It is the duty of the church to remind us that Christians are to give and share generously. One way of doing that is for a "Benevolence Committee" to investigate and recommend charities which are doing a good job and where donations are not wasted. The local parish's responsibility is to encourage and to inform, not to be a surrogate donor. When parishioners themselves decide where and to whom to give more money will flow to needy causes and more parishioners will take an active role in worthwhile charities.

One obstacle to being a "First Hand Samaritan" is the pride churches have in how much they give, *qua* institution, to benevolent agencies. That pride must be replaced by a sense of satisfaction that more individual parishioners are giving more money and giving of their time and talent.

GOD'S TROUBADOURS

In Italian, "Troubadour" is "Il Trovatore": one who composes and sings.

I am certain that my faith would atrophy and become flat if there were no anthems, no hymns, no Bach preludes in church. I cannot conceive of the congregational worship of God without music. My strident monotone still qualifies me as one of God's troubadours. I understand that C.S. Lewis did not like church music. If so, his ears missed much that God had say. Karl Barth, a theological maestro, claimed, not too facetiously, that God created the universe in order for us to hear "The Magic Flute".

American historians are correct when they indicate that the church hymnal has been one of the most formative influences on our national character. Indeed, the first book published in our land was a hymnal, The Bay Psalm Book (1639).

"Why", exclaimed Martin Luther, "should the Devil have all the best tunes?". We have accepted Luther's challenge. The hymnal in my pew has words by Bunyan, Milton, Luther, Samuel Johnson, Chesterton, Kingsley, Oliver W. Holmes, St. Francis, St. Ambrose, Tennyson, Watts, Wesley and Whittier. It has tunes by Bach, Hayden, Beethoven, Orlando Gibbons, Praetorius, Palestrina, Sibelius and Vaughn Williams.

When I was married Purcell's "Voluntary" made the ceremony resonant. When I am buried "Our God, Our Help in Ages Past" will put matters in perspective.

When we worship we sing the "Doxology", from the Greek, meaning to shout a conviction.

In America the oldest hymn in continuous use is that of Timothy Dwight: "I Love Thy Kingdom, Lord" (c.1800). Hymns old and new we sing. Contemporary hymnals are revised to be gender free: "Rise up, O people of God"– not "O Men of God". Choirs lift our hearts. No wonder that Victor Hugo observed that great music expressed that which cannot be said but about which it is impossible to remain silent. I observe that more good music per square mile is heard in churches than in any other places in the United States.

Whether we are singing "The Church's One Foundation" or listening to "Exultate Deo" we are really singing "Lord, speak to me that I may speak in living echoes of thy tone."

GOD'S ALTER EGO

During my exercise class last week a good friend on the adjoining rowing machine slowed his pulse long enough to gasp out, "Have you noticed how much trouble the churches are causing? They give me, I'm sorry, a headache.". He then elaborated with colorful references to headlines about Northern Ireland, creationism, book-censoring, wild cults, greedy evangelists and priestly abusers of children.

My immediate impulse was to set him straight with defensive argument. But candor forced me to reply, "Yes, the church often is a terrible headache." It is true, more times than I care to mention, that the Christian church in its many forms gives society a migraine.

Why does the church cause the headlines which forced the man next to me to pause in his rowing? There are two very embarrassing reasons.

I am the first reason. As an individual Christian I can be a real nuisance. It very well may be that without my faith I would be even worse. But, my ego, my pride and my suspect ambitions are, indeed, a headache both for the church and for the general public. In many ways I think I am a fine fellow; but that doesn't make the headlines. The church is a body of millions of sinning individuals like myself, each of whom boosts aspirin sales.

A second major reason for justifiable complaints about the church is the uncritical habit of some church members, particularly a minority of inflated leaders, to identify the church and its leaders with the will of God, or to insist that the church always speaks clearly for God. These people should be termed God's <u>alter</u> egos.

Here we have a nasty dilemma. The foremost role of the church is to increase devotion to God, to stimulate thought about God and to foster human service on behalf of God. The dilemma arises because focus on those roles creates the devilish temptation to play God.

When the church preens itself with the robes of divinity then institutional pride burgeons, the conditional clauses of theology become hortatory, and theocratic impulses threatens democratic pluralism. Our heads throb the more when the church confuses its interpretation of God's will with national and partisan politics.

Given all that, my exercising friend is right to complain.

There is another side to all this. If only the man on the rowing machine would one day slow down and ask me, "Why do you support the church?". I then guarantee that my reply will send his pulse rate soaring.

A BODILESS CHURCH

Years ago, on a visit to Dartmouth College, I attempted to use its Baker Library for quiet study. I quickly gave up because of the Orozco murals in the reading room. These disconcerting scenes showed the operating ampitheatre of a hospital maternity ward, with skeleton doctors delivering a skeleton mother of a skeleton child. Clustered in the surrounding seats are the dry bone faculty wearing the academic regalia of all the great universities. The mural is a surgical indictment of the type of an educational system that produces stillborn ideas, dead objectivities, inorganic neutralities amid skeletal pomp and circumstance.

The analogous message of the mural for me was that unless the Christian Church in a pluralistic society, in a culture which is polysaturated with threats to Christian values and faith, makes every effort to create support structures it may very well become a skeletal institution. To what degree, for example, can a church survive if it has no support in the school system? If hospitals and city halls and movies and athletic programs and T.V. contain no explicit or implicit support for basic Christian values, it is the height of naivete to think that parish churches can go it alone.

In the early church there was for a short time a heresy called "docetism". Docetists claimed that Christ had no real body; that he only seemed to suffer and die. I submit that modern docetists are Christians who assume that the church can thrive without the help of the body politic or the body educational.

The non-Christian who listens to this plea immediately assumes, with good historical reason, that the church wishes to engage in cultural triumphalism, yearning for theocracy. That I disavow. I do not believe that in the United States any church, faith or ideology can regain a position roughly comparable, let us say, to 17th century American puritanism.

But the Orozco murals still stare us down. To keep flesh on our church bones we need support structures and values in the home, in the school, in civic life and anywhere else we can get it or create it. In that sense the church does not differ from any group with a desire for influence, be it political, educational, artistic, scientific, athletic or religious. There is a real political struggle out there in Main St. There is a cultural competition, a value war. Nonchalant Christian churches, living on past fat, have a dry bone future.

In our pluralistic society how can a church or synagogue find support for their basic values? Must all of such support come from within the church or synagogue? Is a pluralistic society value deaf?

PERIPATETIC PIETY

I read in today's paper that Roman Catholic pilgrimage sites in Europe are booming: at Lourdes, Fatima, Rome and Santiago de Compostela thousands of votive candles are burning. In Spain, the Catholic Church awards a "Pilgrim Certificate" to those faithful who have walked at least 100 kilometers to their pilgrim destination. A French priest accounts for this piety by saying, "People want something more intense, more festive, more emotional."[1] Others note that travel has never been easier, that frequent flier coupons also help.

We American Protestants are not geographical pilgrims. We see life as a pilgrimage from God back to God, but we have no saints, no shrines, no appearances of The Virgin to lure us over land and sea. We have no tradition that seeks salvation wearing a pedometer. I do not denigrate Roman Catholic pilgrimages; I simply record that they are not a Protestant phenomena.

As tourists, we Protestants rejoice in the beauty of Chartres, Canterbury, the Haggia Sophia and St. Peter's. But I do not know of any American Protestant parish which organizes pilgrimages, other than visits to Israel. We are more likely to attend a conference.

We Protestants do not walk for a week expecting to find a miracle or to leave a crutch in a grotto. Where would we go, even if we wished? - to Geneva, Wittenberg, Plymouth Colony, Wesley's room at Oxford? I went to Canterbury to see the steps on which Becket was murdered, not primarily to seek solace for my eternal soul. There is no Lutheran, Presbyterian, Baptist or Episcopal Mecca.

There are, to be sure, many shrines in our land for secular pilgrims: Rockefeller Center, The Golden Gate, the beaches of Hawaii and, above all, far above all, Disney World, the number one tourist attraction in the world. It outdraws St. Peter's, the Grand Canyon and The Tower of London.

So, where does the Protestant pilgrim go? The credit card is of no avail. We seek our God in our parish church, in private prayer, on a retreat. We are stay-at-home Christians. We are "pilgrims to the interior", not to the exterior.

Sir Walter Raleigh depicted the nature of his mobile pilgrimage in these lovely lines:

> "Give me my scallop-shell of quiet,
> My staff of faith to walk upon.
> My scrip of joy, immortal diet,
> My bottle of salvation,
> My gown of glory, hope's true gage,
> And thus I'll take my pilgrimage."

We Protestants, to the contrary, nourish our faith wherever we are. God and Christ are as close on Main Street as at Rome or Lourdes.

---

1. N.Y. Times, 10/12/93

ON BEING AN AMERICAN CHRISTIAN

"America! America!
God shed his grace on thee.
And crown thy good with brotherhood
From sea to shining sea!"

If written today, Katherine Lee Bates would have made her patriotic hymn gender-inclusive. Her hymn is cited because it is a familiar example of the Siamese-twin bonding between American Christianity and the political history of our nation. This close intimacy of faith and civil tradition has given to American Christianity its star-spangled coloration. American Christians are no exception to the manner in which the faith of Christians in all nations reflects the ethos and traditions of their native countries.

The particularity of American Christianity is most clearly visible when American Christians, both clergy and laity, are transplanted to an alien national setting. For some thirty summers, off and on, I had the opportunity of observing American Christians in just such a background. I served as Director of summer schools for American clergy and laity at Oxford, St. Andrews, Rome and Montreux. The American attributes were unmistakable when contrasted and compared with the various European churches and their parishioners.

American Christian characteristics are of the following sort: There is a vigorous, gregarious optimism of character. Hope abounds that all will go well if only enough people had the benefits of liberal democracy, freedom and technology. One American form of agape is a cordial handshake. There is no simplistic, naive ideology of progress, but there is an affirmation of life coupled with the energy to seek the better life.

The American Christian is clearly uneasy about and baffled by national established churches, many of which are distressingly weak. The usual observation of American Christians about such churches is: "If those churches were self supporting, with parishioners who have to find and cultivate members, such churches would come to life". Similarly, American Christians are undoubtedly more supportive of philanthropies and foundations, not expecting the central government to do it all.

If my antennae are accurate, I further perceive American laity to be much less suspicious about and generally more affirming of the clergy than in nations with established churches.

American Christians are high decibel worshippers and singers. An American church shouts. A Swiss or Scottish church whispers.

I am not making comparative value judgements. Were I doing so, I would list the strengths of European churches. I am simply describing the tone and feel of the American Christian, while admitting that generalizations easily become caricatures.

In any event, it would take the fingers of a brain surgeon to separate out in the mind of the American Christian the national and the theological synapses. The American Christian has been produced by the slow alchemy of separation of church and state, denominational competition, religious liberty, political freedom and the American Dream.

Of late, I notice a new nervousness mixing with the usual gregarious, activistic and optimistic nature of American Christians. We are finding it more difficult to handle the noisy, aggressive religious diversity in America. For example, Muslim mosques next to McDonalds, Mormon missionaries in suburbia, New Age disciples, exotic cults and ethnic resurgence. Also, the wars and traumas of our era are tempering the ethical meliorism of American Protestants.

The crucial issue remains. Can American Christians maintain a healthy lover's quarrel with their native land, making certain that patriotism does not co-opt and camouflage their faith?

A GOOD WORD FOR DO-GOODERS

Given the thin veneer of civilization, I applaud anyone who is intelligently attempting to improve matters. I regret how often do-gooders have been the target of satire. Mark Twain wrote that if he knew anyone was coming after him to do him good, he would flee instantly. He had been subjected as a child to a heavy dose of moralizing. I can understand his anxiety.

Doing good badly is a moral boomerang. An unattractive personality does not harmonize with good actions. Nor does the person who does good on a <u>quid pro quo</u>, back-scratching basis. Self-righteous do-gooders stab themselves. Starchy do-gooders bring to mind the visit which Abraham Lincoln endured when a delegation of stiff-necked clergy came to set him straight on his ethics. After their departure, Lincoln told his aide the story of a small boy who sculpted a beautiful church out of mud, a church filled with pews and a pulpit. When asked, "Where's the preacher?", the boy replied, "I ran out of mud.".

After all necessary concessions have been made to critics of do-gooders, I still maintain, knowing a vast number of laity and clergy who have "done good well", that their host far outnumbers those who morally are all thumbs.

I have been so gratefully impressed over and again by the quiet, self-effacing, untrumpeted do-gooding that goes on in season and out. There is good reason to believe that much of our world is held together by those who do good without looking for merit badges or expecting the audience to call for an encore.

VOX POPULI, VOX DEI?

I lived for a dozen years in Princeton, New Jersey, the home office of the famous Gallup Poll. Several Gallup employees were prominent members of our parish church. At one congregational meeting the main item for discussion was (as usual): "The Need to Increase Membership". One Gallup parishioner began the discussion by maintaining that the surest way to increase membership would be to poll the present members, asking them to answer this question: "What do you want the church to be and do?". The results of that poll, it was argued, should be the church's agenda. When carried out, that program would produce a steady influx of new members.

The debate which followed that proposal was a strident commentary on the often quoted but seldom followed aphorism: "The Voice of the People Is the Voice of God".

One one side were those who reacted with horror to such a Gallupian ecclesiology. These members passionately contended that The Bible, the great creeds and church tradition were not to be tinkered with so cavalierly. Their assumption was that a purely democratically produced agenda for church life would lead to heresy. Their contention essentially was that the voice of God is determined by a selected few.

The "Gallupers" rose to their feet, on the other side, to question such uncritical obedience to past church councils, theologians, creeds and clergy. There is a validity to a voting majority - at the very least, it must be heard. Translated into commercial jargon, the pollsters asserted that the customer is usually right and that the parish programs should be user friendly. They objected to a church too much controlled by Protestant Prelates (lay or ordained) and by the heavy hand of unexamined tradition.

I now conclude, from this distance, that in such a church debate there is one loser and one winner.

The biggest loser is the very phrase "Vox Populi, Vox Dei". It should not ever be employed by a church, by a congregation or by an individual. It is idolatry.

The winner is any minister or church which sensitively seeks to balance the contributions of Christian scholarship, church tradition and congregational desire. The balancing act is always precarious, never perfect.

THE CLERGY

"One of the saddest things I have had to do is counsel those who have drifted into ordination in a haze of idealism. They failed to count the cost. Ordination should be embraced only as a passion and not undertaken as a meal ticket or a career ...."

Alan Jones, <u>Sacrifice and Delight</u>

A WORD TO AND FROM THE PULPIT

During the customary Protestant Sunday worship the sermon occupies about a third of the time. The balance is divided between music, prayers, scripture, offertory and announcements. This time-sharing clearly gives a favored place to the sermon. The unavoidable implication for the preacher is to be interesting, understandable and relevant. To fail that challenge is fatal. An anecdote about President Coolidge makes the point: on coming out of church in Northampton, Massachusetts, he was asked by a reporter, "What did the minister preach about?" The pithy reply was, "He didn't say."

The pulpit message will not penetrate through the ear to the intellect and to the emotions unless the words catch and hold attention. Two minutes of a dull beginning will cause those in the pews to wonder how long it is to tee-time or why the front lawn is turning brown.

The sermon must shake the worshipper, saying forcefully, "This gospel is about you and your world.".

Sermons are packaged in many styles: the expository/exegetical, the situation/life centered, the assigned/lectionary, the extemporaneous, or in varying combinations. Each style (and substance) can be preached well or poorly. I, for instance, do poorly with an assigned/lectionary schedule which mandates each sermon's scripture and topic. An obligatory sermon text may not be one that moves and interests me. Unless I am stirred, the sermon will limp.

The congregation has every right to expect a thoughtful, moving sermon which give evidence of serious preparation. An off-the-cuff sermon is a burnt offering.

My own path to ordination was widened and lighted by a generation of superb preachers of winning power and persuasion. The preachers embodied theological and biblical depth with personal fire.

God and Christ come alive in fine sermons in a manner that no other medium of worship can surpass - equal with Scripture, Sacrament, prayer and music.

A sermon which does not win the attention of the congregation is a clear indication either that the minister has not done the homework or that he or she is in the wrong vocation. A listless preacher spawns sermon-phobia.

MINISTERIAL MOBILITY

How long should a parish minister stay in a local parish? There may be churches or denominations which enforce arbitrary terms of office, with mandated departure times. If there are such, I do not know of them. I do recall that in rural America the Methodist Church at one time had a regular three year rotation scheme. It was said in those days that when the minister came home from the Annual Conference the chickens would lie down to have their feet tied.

Pastoral mobility is constant, but there seems to be no formula or criterion which determines fairly how long a minister should remain in one place.

I understand that football coaches average seven years on the gridirons. College faculty with tenure enjoy more settled futures. The clergy, unlike the coaches, have no won-loss statistics and, unlike tenured faculty, they have no guaranteed support system.

I once played tennis regularly with a surgeon. One day he told me that he had just retired. I asked why he had done so. His reply was that his colleagues told him that his hands and nerves no longer were passing muster. My tennis partner accepted their verdict as an unarguable professional courtesy.

Such candor is seldom found in the parish. Congregations are often too permissive, being reluctant in the name of compassion and friendship to tell the minister that it is time to go...to say that his or her mind and energy, like the surgeon's, were no longer able to pass muster.

Clergy have widely differing opinions about the optimal stay in a parish. I have heard the matter debated thoroughly. A minority claim that five years is a minimum if trust is to be won, people known and programs carried forward. I myself posit ten to twelve years as the desirable time span. I know, however, several ministers who have done superbly over twenty five years, just as there are too many churches which are bored to tears with clergy who have stayed too long.

No matter how short or long the duration of a ministry, each and every minister who decides to move-on, to accept a "Call", needs to ask two basic questions, standing in front of the mirror of self.

First: Am I too glibly equating my desire to go elsewhere with the "Will of God"? Is the "Will of God" a pious phrase being used to justify moving for other reasons? How does one know, anyway, the "Will of God" on such a matter?

In other words, is not honesty better served by saying, "I wish to move because I need more money", or "I accept the invitation of the First Church of Beulah because I and my family need a change and a new challenge".

Second: Is my desire to accept another church's offer really a dodge for avoiding the real problem? That is, I say to myself that I am tired of my parish and that I need a greener pasture. But what I am not admitting is that the minute I get to the next parish I am still tired of parish routine. If such is the case, I need counseling.

Any minister who moves too opportunistically leaves behind what in the sport pages is called a "losing season".

SEX AND SERMONS

If my barrel of old sermons is valid evidence, I find that I have never preached about sex. I have written about sex; I have lectured about it, led seminars on "Sex Ethics" and, more to the point, I have enjoyed sex. However, I have never had any desire to preach on that subject, and I have never had a request to do so.

This gap in homiletical subject matter is not due to my underestimation of the power and role of sex in our lives. I am as familiar as most with the energy of sex in body, mind, soul and id. As John Barrymore said, "Sex takes less time and causes more trouble than any other human activity."

Given the unhappy attitude toward sex in too much church history, I blush at my sermonic negligence. Surely I should have used the pulpit to correct the dreary Christian tradition which conjoined intercourse with original sin. This resulted in chastity being elevated above marriage in the scale of virtue. St. Paul was not too comfortable about his libido. I am told that Francis of Assisi would jump into snow banks to cool off his wandering thoughts. I caricature, but not by much. Too many Christian traditions smothered normal sex with crippling taboos. There was, in short, plenty in Christian history to merit sermonic rectification.

Therefore, I list my reasons for avoiding the subject of sex in the pulpit. I hope these are not rationalizations.

Reason One: We are so erotically supersaturated that the congregation listening to a sermon about sex would pay little attention. Every conceivable forms of sexual behavior inundates us in the media. To preach about sex is the equivalent of running the garden hose in a rain forest. Is there anything sexual that ninety-nine percent of the congregation has not heard on the psychiatric couch, seen in movies or T.V. or read about in newspaper and books? Only this week I gulped only a slight gulp to read in "Harper's" a symposium of four college teachers affirming that there is no valid reason why faculty and students should not cohabit, if agreement is mutual.

Reason Two: In the pews there is a mixture of adults and minors, the old and the young, the divorced, the happily married, the unmarried, homosexuals (in the closet or out). What sermonic net can be cast that will catch all that variety of sexuality?

Reason Three: All the churches, all the denominations with which I am acquainted, are in the throes of debate about the role, place and nature of "Christian sexuality". There are debates which rock and shock. The Bible is quoted pro and con. Good Christians are living together out of wedlock, who a few years back could have been looked at with horror. Churches advocate mature love, caring and responsibility in sex. But it is a "situation ethic" run riot. I am not confident enough to preach guidelines.

Those three reasons might validate my decision to refrain from preaching about sex. I am not sure that they are sufficient reasons. Were I doing it again, perhaps I would change my mind.

In a church setting, I suggest that the most effective way to discuss and discover a Christian view of sex is in Sunday School, in seminars, in confirmation class, in adult forms - especially in settings where the laity speak up.

I do surmise, of course, that there are clergy who preach about sex. Power to them. I pass.

MY REAL BIBLE

My working edition of The Holy Bible contains 1622 pages, including the Apocrypha. Far more than any other writings, I have studied those biblical pages with diligence and with scholarly aids. My faith, my ordination, is anchored in the Bible.

Now, years later and after all that attention, I realize to my dismay that my real Bible, those portions to which I have given the closest thought, is but a minority of those 1622 pages, perhaps six or seven hundred pages. As I thumb through the texts of my sermons and my biblically oriented writings it is chastening to discover how many sections of the Bible I have slighted.

My personal Bible, that is, is to be found in those books, chapters and verses on which I have based my most meaningful Christian convictions. Such selectivity is true of every Christian.

I have never, of course, regarded everything in the Bible as having equal value. Nevertheless, I do find it disturbing to realize how limited has been my utilization of the full riches of the Bible.

Naturally, in one ministerial career with many responsibilities, there is bound to be a partial use of the Bible. I have concentrated on those portions of scripture which resonate most personally. Even lectionary sermonizers, even teachers of the Bible, have their own truncated bibles.

There is nothing wrong with biblical selectivity. It is not a reason for guilt. It is, however, an occasion for reflection. Have I omitted major themes and narratives? Have I skewed the biblical text because of personal bias? Is there more isogesis than exegesis? Have I presented to the church a Bible lacking its full power and majesty?

THE CHRISTIAN:

PROFESSIONAL AND AMATEUR

I vacated my amateur Christian standing when I entered Yale Divinity School. I was thereby on my way to becoming a professional Christian. Graduate study, plus ordination, officially confirmed my professional status. Theoretically, being a professional means that I am competent in a field of specialized knowledge and practice, that I am more concerned with my occupation that with monetary award, that I am acceptable to my church and my other professional colleagues and that I am a member of a self-policing in-group. If I desire to show off, I can express my professional status with the vocabulary and pass words peculiar to my trade.

"Professional" should not be a pejorative. At best, it indicates the application of competence to community service. Being a serious professional is to fill a worthy role. Professionalism need not automatically result in arrogance, in pride of office or in looking down on "amateur" Christians. Being a professional Christian certainly should not merit the quip of H.L. Mencken: "A minister is someone who has attained to a higher status than Jesus Christ." No, much of our civilization is strengthened by professionals in law, medicine, divinity, teaching and business.

As a professional Christian, how do I differ from the amateur? I only can guess at the answer because I am no longer able to see the gospel and the church with the peculiar vision of the amateur. My chief surmise about the amateur Christian is that they are freer disciples than I. I have obligations to the church, to the society of colleagues and to my daily ministerial duties. I also wish to remain eligible for the church pension fund.

The amateur Christian is freer to wander about, probably more inclined to go it alone. The amateur is not tightly beholden to the routine expectations in a congregation or to a fixed role. Amateur Christians earn their faith without the many forms of assistance given the professional.

Because of my professional education I can quote chapter and verse, cite Augustine or Barth or the latest interpretation of the Kingdom of God. I wear dignifying robes. I am surrounded with ritualistic symbols. On the contrary, the amateur functions without the symbols, disciplines and privileges of the professional.

As a freer person, less subject to ecclesiastical scrutiny, the amateur usually is forgiven more lapses in faith and in morals. Fairly or not, the professional Christian is held on a tighter and shorter leash. Moral deviation or theological wanderings are to be kept at a respectable minimum.

However, when sincerity and hypocrisy, faithfulness and backsliding are balanced in the scales of judgement, I cannot rank either the amateur or the professional as the better Christian. It is an individual not a group evaluation that must be made.

As a professional disciple, I am eager to salute and admire the amateur disciples in full recognition of their accomplishments.

ONE ARMED JUSTICE

One of the continuing frustrations about the ministry is how difficult it is to help shape a congregation for effective leadership in matters of social and political justice.

Before too much <u>mea culpa</u> confession, however, I do wish to say that I am thoroughly convinced that the gospel is inseparable from the pursuit of social justice: love and justice are siblings. I have been active in a variety of political and social betterment activities. I have never advocated a quietistic piety.

Nevertheless, I am baffled about leading effectively a local congregation into a program with real clout in matters of extra-church justice. Therefore, I wish to list factors which severely limit the influence of a local minister and a local congregation in matters pertaining to commonwealth justice:

1. Many parishioners have trouble, in practice if not in theory, in giving social justice equal priority with personal faith development. This self-regard is understandable, since most of the time each of us is the center of the universe.

2. The minister, however fervent his or her desire for programs of justice, spends most of the available time and energy in nourishing, in keeping alive and growing the local parish.

3. There is always a tense diversity of opinion within a congregation on social and political issues. The parish is political animal of and by itself.

4. Laity and clergy shy away from controversy.

5. Political action takes time and money.

6. IRS restrictions on tax exempt churches put limits on actions regarded as political partisan.

The obvious result of these restraints is that local churches and their clergy tend to limit themselves to "ambulance care" measures: tending the wounded rather than getting rid of the forces which cause the wounds. I refer to such good works as soup kitchens, shelters for the homeless, Thanksgiving and Christmas charity, working with "habitats", etc.

Judicatory bodies of churches and denominations give careful thought and debate in framing "Resolutions" advocating just measures in such matters as Aids, women's rights, refugees, ecology. These manifestos add momentum in the right direction but too often end up floating in the still pond of public apathy.

I continue to lament that we Christians, both Protestant and Catholic, do not have more influence for the good, fair and honorable in public affairs. The six reasons listed above are not, however, excuses for lack of courage.

THE MINISTER'S FATAL SIN

It is hard for a young person about to be ordained to be fully aware of personal hubris and sin. At such a moment one is full of ideals and visions and the face of God in Jesus Christ. One's own serious sins and failures are not so close to the skin of conscience.

Early in my parish ministry I reckoned (with unbelievable naivete) that my worst ministerial error would be a sermonic dud.

Later on, I admitted the graver error of forgetting that I was married to my wife rather than to the church. I was not the "Groom" of Christ. Another error, further along toward maturity, was the neglect of personal devotional life. Because I knew much theology, was busy with admirable parish chores and Sunday worship it was tempting to believe that I was devotional enough, pious enough. The opposite was the truth: the more "professional" I was, the greater the need for quiet, disciplined devotion.

Another error, not a sin, caused aggravation: namely, inattention to administrative details. I think of sloppy staff meetings, of important correspondence glibly handled, of committee meetings attended with an addled mind. Nor shall I ever forget the time I missed a Baptism. The parents, too, have never forgotten.

At this remove, looking over my shoulder and into my heart, I know that the worst failure or sin of a minister is to behave in word or deed in such a manner as to lose the trust and respect of parishioners. With diligence, it takes two or three years to win affectionate trust. It takes only one foolhardy sin such as serious dishonesty to lose that regard.

It is all very well for the erring minister to plead that he or she is only human and in need of forgiveness. Forgiveness, indeed, may be forthcoming, but the bitter fact of ordained life is that when trust has been broken other accomplishments or other virtues will not compensate.

This astringent warning needs an analogy. A ballet dancer, who also is human, but who constantly falls down flat-footed, is dismissed from the company. Apologies will not suffice. Nor will personal attractiveness. There simply are certain acts, similarly, which fatally undercut one's ordained ministry. Anyone contemplating ordination should, as the Book of Common Prayer enjoins, "read, mark, learn and inwardly digest" this valid warning to all clergy.

> "This little proverb he would add thereto
> That if gold rust what then will iron do?
> For if a priest be foul in whom we trust
> No wonder that a common man should rust."
>
> (Chaucer: Canterbury Tales)

A CHRISTIAN COMMENCEMENT

I write this in the midst of the collegiate Commencement season. Now is the time for the awarding of honorary degrees. I was pleased, therefore, that by coincidence I recently ran across in <u>The Oxford Dictionary of the Christian Church</u> a listing of "Doctors, Scholastic". Instead of honorary degrees these eminent Christians were given distinguished titles. here are a few, translated from the Latin:

> Thomas Aquinas: Angelic Doctor
> Roger Bacon: Miraculous Doctor
> Giovanni Bonaventura: Seraphic Doctor
> William of Ockham: Invincible Doctor
> Duns Scotus: Subtle Doctor
> Jan Van Ruysbroek: Ecstatic Doctor

Seeing no reason why such meritocracy should not continue beyond The late Middle Ages, I submit the following 20th Century "Divines" for Commencement degrees, <u>honoris causa:</u>

> Mary Baker Eddy: Immaterial Doctor
> Reinhold Niebuhr: Paradoxical Doctor
> Richard Niebuhr: Exemplary Doctor
> Billy Graham: Media Doctor
> Mary Daly: Female Doctor
> Wilhelm Visser Hooft: Ecumenical Doctor
> Karl Barth: Transcendent Doctor
> Pope John Paul II: Dogmatic Doctor
> Dietrich Bonoeffer: Martyred Doctor

Rosemary Reuther: Liberated Doctor
Dorothy Day: Ghetto Doctor
Paul Tillich: Ultimate Doctor
William Sloane Coffin: Front Line Doctor

The reader is invited to add and to modify.

CONTINUING COMPETENCE

Henry James once was lured as a visiting lecturer to the famous New York Chatauqua, the vacation center for religious and cultural uplift. A week proved to be the limit of the elegant jamesian endurance. He wrote to his philosopher brother, William: "Never have I met so many earnest but helpless minds".

I quote that as an introduction to this plea for the continuing cultural and religious education of the clergy. We clergy are for the most part earnest and conscientious, but we are not helpless and we do not wish to be outdated professionals. I say that because more and more denominations and local parishes are providing continuing education sabbaticals for the clergy. That is very good news, indeed. All professionals - doctors, lawyers, teachers, et al who do not benefit from good continuing education soon become obsolete. A cheerful personality, visible piety and honorific regard will not substitute for serious post-ordination education.

The continuing education of which I speak has several crucial components: (1) It is long and recurring enough to make a solid impact on the heart and mind, (2) It is primarily designed by the clergy themselves, (3) It is in addition to the normal annual vacation and synodical cabals, (4) It has guaranteed financing, usually in an annual escrow line budget, (5) It is preceded by a counseling and advisory process which enables the minister to ascertain genuine personal and professional needs.

The best model for clerical continuing education is that of the collegiate system which underwrites periodic sabbaticals as a prime method of stimulating academic competence and esprit.

Apart from such sabbaticals, even the most motivated minister can barely keep up with religious thought and cultural creativity. The weekly responsibilities leave precious little time for significant study. Obsolescence always threatens.

So it is that today thousands of churches write into the contract with the minister that the parish is responsible for effective continuing education and that the local church expects the minister to keep growing intellectually and spiritually. Such arrangements are not fringe benefits, they are evangelical necessities.

I think that a minimum sabbatical leave is three months, every five or six years, the very least in which a minister can settle down and dig deeply enough.

This educational stewardship implies that the clergy, educated at such cost, take to heart the Commencement Season exhortation that "Now your education is ready to begin". Competent professionalism and education are siblings. If they do not stay together, the church suffers as much as the minister.

As I look around at the types of sabbaticals taken by clergy, I am cheered and impressed by the variety: back to seminary, digging in at Oxford, soaking up Rome, visiting interesting churches and parishes, a series of Elderhostels, retreating to a rural setting with a study program in mind, university based continuing education, writing a book. The key criterion for a worthwhile sabbatical is to do whatever will cause the blood to flow and the brain to click and at the same time have feedback value for the home church.

It is regrettable, of course, that too many churches cannot afford to underwrite both a sabbatical for the minister and a salary for the interim. In most cases, I suspect, the financial goal can be met once there is a mutual realization by minister and parish that each will gain strength from continuing education.

GREENER FIELDS AND

MINISTERIAL SALARIES

A New England church, not to be identified, was announcing a special Lenten Preacher. On the church's outdoor bulletin board were these words underneath the minister's name: "The Highest Paid Minister in New England."

My sarcastic laugh was followed by the realization that the sponsoring church was being open and honest about what is a widespread but more discreetly voiced policy: namely, if a church wants top leadership it has to pay for it and outbid the competition. In that sense, what is good for General Motors is good for a parish. My sarcasm is also muted by the undoubted fact that I, too, have profited from this bidding war. I won a few and lost a few. I do not intend to bite the hand that fed me; but I do wish to press for an alternative strategy for ministerial remuneration.

The issue which needs a new strategy is defined by this question: "To what extent should salary level determine a minister's choice of church-related occupation"?

I have never seen accurate statistics on the subject, but I am willing to bet a year's salary that at least 90% of American Protestant clergy leave one post for another only if there is a salary increase. Further, I warrant that, if salary were not the issue, most ministers would seek parishes and positions where they genuinely wished to be rather than accepting a new "Call" primarily to secure better pay. For example, I know of ministers who love small, rural parishes but who are forced to seek for larger churches in order to cover family expenses as the years go by. One unhappy result of such a system is that more and more ministers fall into the habit of equating God's will with a call to a better paid and greener pasture. In any event, the connection between money, motivation and place of occupation needs very serious scrutiny.

My alternative proposal is that a few denominations initiate a "Salary Equalization System", comparable to that in the military, the Civil Service, universities, and in some corporations. The churches can find no exact analogy elsewhere, but a Salary Equalization System would provide predictability of income over the years and centralization of financial operation (as with a pension fund). A list of variables would be established: age, education, experience, size of family, etc. with varying salaries for various stages. There would be a spread between minimal and maximum incomes, but the main objective is two-fold: (1) to provide an adequate minimal income and (2) to help clergy make occupational moves that are based more on personal desire than on income.

I realize that the American entrepreneurial system has such a strong hold on church Trustees that it is very hard to resist a bidding war. Years ago Congressman Jack Kemp was asked, "What would happen if Babe Ruth's salary had been equal to all other Yankees?". The reply was, "He would hit singles!".

I am not willing to admit that the better paid clergy are the best. Nor am I going to deny that some clergy are better than others. However, we really should examine any assumption that makes an easy correlation between size of income and effective Christian discipleship.

In this brief plea there is no room for detailed analysis of various actuarial and administrative blueprints by which to implement a Salary Equalization System. Nor do I wish to make this a strident <u>ideé fixe</u>. But it does merit discussion, debate and, I hope, implementation somewhere.

BENEFIT OF CLERGY

The words "Benefit of Clergy" began in Europe centuries ago. It referred to the legal right of clergy to be exempt from civil tribunals, even in acts of felony. Jurisdiction of clergy was given to church courts. In England that practice did not cease until 1827.

I have received many "Benefits of Clergy", more by virtue of ordination than by personal merit.

I recall that in the 1950's there was a kind of K-Mart discount club for clergy. A small annual membership fee provided me a twenty percent discount on anything from lawnmowers to bird-food. Several times I have been granted low cost membership in clubs. I have benefited from the mercy of the cop who caught me speeding, asking for my driver's license, saw "Rev." and waved me on. My clergy status has brought me front row seats at crowded public and private gatherings, without waiting in the ticket line. The text for all of these benefits is Matthew 23:6: "They love to have the place of honor at banquets and the best seats in the synagogues".

One questionable benefit is the frequent sanitized conversation initiated by those seated next to me on a plane and who, upon discovering my profession, immediately tell me how religious they are "even though I don't go to church".

All of the above cited privileges are only fringe benefits, some appreciated, some resented, some patronizing.

The genuine benefits of clergy are of an altogether different genre. I refer to the deep and refreshing friendships, to the intimate confidences where the joys and sorrows of life are shared. I refer to the privilege of leading public worship. I appreciate enormously the time permitted for study, conjoined with the challenge that I try to be a well informed, persuasive and relevant ambassador for God and Christ.

Thankfully, of course, many walks of life other than the ministry have benefits peculiar to them: lawyers, teachers, doctors, public servants, business leaders, craftsmen and artists.

And, alas, far too many lives experience few benefits beyond mere existence.

So, fellow clergy, discount any fringe benefits and count with gratitude the genuine.

FIFTY YEARS A MINISTER

A Sermon preached at
The Round Hill Community Church
Greenwich, Connecticut

FIFTY YEARS A MINISTER

Scriptures: Ecclesiasticus 51:19b:

"I spread out my hands to the Heavens, and lamented my ignorance of her."

Colossians 1:15b:

"He is the image of the invisible God."

An anniversary occasion such as this is a dangerous time. Fifty years in the ministry has provided me with enough pulpit ammunition to have you begging for surrender and yearning for the closing hymn.

Please be at ease. I will spare you the pulpit buckshot and remind myself that no one lasts fifty years in the ministry by preaching too long.

Since I was ordained in January, 1945, I have had the good fortune to be in a variety of positions: Marine Corps chaplaincy, college chaplaincies at Yale, Colby and Northwestern, foundation director, seminary administrator in parishes in Hartford and Greenwich. That very variety, in preparing this sermon, made for this question: *In all of those ministries are there one or two prevailing themes which animated me, which I feel are important, and which are worth your attention?*

At this time I certainly do not wish to speak about anecdotes. This is not the time to mention the wedding here in Greenwich where the groom fainted twice. Nor is this pulpit the place to recall my first summer parish, in 1945 in rural Michigan, soy bean country. After that worship service the head deacon came up and asked me in a portentous voice: "Are you saved?" I have never asked that of anyone since. Nor is this the proper moment to tell you of a communion service in Hartford when the sexton came up to me afterwards and handed me a set of brass knuckles found in the pews. Here in Greenwich I was never that persuasive!

But enough of such nostalgia.

Now I do seek your serious consideration to two issues which have been the most challenging to me over all these years as a minister. They are major motifs, and I wish to share them with you.

The first issue is the healthy tension between my Christian convictions and my human ignorance. This tension affects both you and me, but it is especially acute in the lives of the clergy because in our teaching and preaching our voices often sound omniscient, as if our minds had no limits, no ignorance. Let me elaborate.

As a follower of Christ, I affirm creeds about God, Jesus, values, life , death and destiny. These affirmations led me to ordination. As a minister, I talk and teach constantly about God, but I am human, and I voice these convictions about a universe and God and Christ I cannot fully comprehend. As I read from the Book of Ecclesiasticus: "I spread out my hands to the Heavens, and lamented my ignorance of her." I am tightly wedged between my enthusiastic convictions about God and Christ on the one hand and, on the other, the unrelenting knowledge that I am not God and cannot know it all.

The very important point is that we be aware of this tension between Christian conviction and human finiteness. This awareness is healthy; it is stimulating, and it keeps us in our proper size.

We Christians are not alone in this predicament. All interpreters of the human situation, be they religious or non-religious, share in this tension between conviction and ignorance: the Christian, the Jew, the Muslim, the atheist.

I confess, therefore, to being very unhappy about any organization, any religion which claims with absolute finality to know it all. I am very uncomfortable with any who take God into cozy partnership.

On the other hand, I enjoy immensely those thinkers, scientists, artists, theologians who love to debate life's meaning and who do so with the fitting admission that they don't have the final answers.

"I spread out my hands to the Heavens, and lamented my ignorance of her."

The other, the second life-long, tension is this. How can I arrive at a final, conclusive portrayal of Jesus of Nazareth and his relationship to God? That is another profitable tension that both animates and frustrates me.

Here is the issue: There is no one full and final portrait of Jesus in the New Testament. Each Gospel, each letter writer, paints a portrait from a different personal perspective. As has been well put, we do not have an historical photograph of Jesus: we have a set of paintings, of slightly differing interpretations.

Over the years since 1945, I have been studying these portraits of Jesus in the hope that I will see him more clearly as he really was.

There is, of course, no doubt about how the vast majority of Christian churches have interpreted the New Testament Jesus. All of the great creeds make the same central claim: that what we see, who we see in the New Testament is the unique revealer of the nature and purpose of God. My own way of phrasing that is to assert that the spirit, teaching, life and death and resurrection of Jesus are our best clues to the nature and purpose of God.

Having affirmed that, it still has to be reiterated that no one portrait of Jesus will suffice. Scholars and non-scholars constantly amend and shade those New Testament portraits. As we learn more about biblical times, culture, archeology and language we are forced to see Jesus in a new light. I have never been satisfied with any one portrait and never shall be. And yet I still say,

"He is the image of the invisible God."

You know as well as I that there are many who look at the New Testament portraits of Jesus and see there only a prophet or a Jewish Socrates, an important and attractive figure, but not the most decisive or normative.

I myself must admit that I often have resented Jesus. He constantly interferes with things I like to do or should have done. My world is filled with other competing sirens. If I had only my own pleasure to consider, I would pick a less demanding savior.

But there Jesus is in those new Testament portraits. He catches my eye and beguiles my heart as no other. More telling, when I look at him he looks through me and knows me.

Such, Dear Friends, are the two tensions which have played a major role in my ministry. In this church we live with these tensions and profit from them.

I repeat: if we do not admit our final ignorance, we become religious prigs or bigots. If we do not find life's finest religious convictions, we will drift into the doldrums without anchor or compass.

And so I say and so I affirm: even in our final ignorance we, because of Jesus, have compelling reason to believe in a good God. In all the varying portraits of Jesus, what and who we see is clear and commanding.

My concluding word is this. The best portion of fifty years in the ministry is not where I began, but where I am today, here with you in this lovely church. Ralph and Lynne are superb ministers. In fifty years I have never seen or known a more supportive congregation of friends. Fafie joins hands with me, as we join hands with you. We are pilgrims together. And so I say, Amen, with love.

> Delivered by Walter D. Wagoner,
> January 15, 1995.

This world is not conclusion;
A sequel stands beyond.
Invisible, as music,
But positive, as sound.
It beckons and it baffles;
Philosophies don't know,
And through a riddle, at the last,
Sagacity, must go.
To guess it puzzles scholars;
To gain it, men have shown
Contempt of generations,
And crucifixion known.

       Emily Dickinson

Walter D. Wagoner is an ordained minister in the United Church of Christ. He has held several pastorates in Connecticut, in addition to being a chaplain at Colby College, at Northwestern University and in the United States Marine Corps. He has also been the Director of the Rockefeller Brothers Fund for Theological Education, the Director of the Boston Theological Institute, and the Associate Dean of the Graduate Theological Union in Berkeley, California. He was a member of the 1962-1963 committee that reviewed Yale's undergraduate Department of Religion.

Dr. Wagoner holds a B.A. degree (1941) from Yale University and a B.D. degree (1945) from Yale Divinity School. He earned his Th.M. at Princeton Seminary and has done further graduate studies at the University of Chicago. He also holds honorary degrees from College of the Holy Cross in Massachusetts and McGill University in Montreal, Canada and the Pacific School of Religion in California.

The Reverend Walter Wagoner is the founder of American Summer Institute Schools in Oxford, St. Andrews, Rome and Montreux..

Prior to the publication of this book, Dr. Wagoner has authored several books, including *Bittersweet Grace, Unity in Mid-Career, Bachelor of Divinity* and *The Seminary: Protestant and Catholic*. Three collections of his sermons have also been published: *Mortgages on Paradise, Say a Good Word for Jesus* and *Round Hill Sermons*.